For Lizzie and Harriet

ROBERT LOWELL

For Lizzie and Harriet

FABER & FABER
3 Queen Square London

First published in 1973
by Faber and Faber Limited
3 Queen Square London WC1
Printed in Great Britain by
W & J Mackay Limited Chatham

ISBN 0 571 10296 4

Note

In another order, in other versions, all the
poems in this book appeared in my last
published poem, *Notebook*.

Contents

For Lizzie and Harriet

Summer

1. *Harriet, born January 4, 1957*

Half a year, then a year and a half, then
ten and a half—the pathos of a child's fractions, turn-
ing up each summer. Her God a seaslug, God a queen
with forty servants, God—you gave up . . . things whirl
in the chainsaw bite of whatever squares
the universe by name and number. For
the hundredth time, we slice the fog, and round
the village with our headlights on the ground,
like the first philosopher Thales who thought all things water,
and fell in a well . . . trying to find a car
key. . . . It can't be here, and so it must be there
behind the next crook in the road or growth
of fog—there blinded by our feeble beams,
a face, clock-white, still friendly to the earth.

2. *Harriet*

A repeating fly, blueback, thumbthick—so gross,
it seems apocalyptic in our house—
whams back and forth across the nursery bed
manned by a madhouse of stuffed animals,
not one a fighter. It is like a plane
dusting apple orchards or Arabs on the screen—
one of the mighty . . . one of the helpless. It
bumbles and bumps its brow on this and that,
making a short, unhealthy life the shorter.
I kill it, and another instant's added
to the horrifying mortmain of
ephemera: keys, drift, sea-urchin shells,
you packrat off with joy . . . a dead fly swept
under the carpet, wrinkling to fulfillment.

3. *Elizabeth*

An unaccustomed ripeness in the wood;
move but an inch and moldy splinters fall
in sawdust from the walls' aluminum-paint,
once loud and fresh, now aged to weathered wood.
Squalls of the seagull's exaggerated outcry
dim out in the fog. . . . *Pace, pace*. All day our words
were rusty fish-hooks—wormwood . . . Dear Heart's-Ease,
we rest from all discussion, drinking, smoking,
pills for high blood, three pairs of glasses—soaking
in the sweat of our hard-earned supremacy,
offering a child our leathery love. We're fifty,
and free! Young, tottering on the dizzying brink
of discretion once, you wanted nothing,
but to be old, do nothing, type and think.

4. *These Winds*   (*Harriet*)

I see these winds, these are the tops of trees,
these are no heavier than green alder bushes;
touched by a light wind, they begin to mingle
and race for instability—too high placed
to stoop to the strife of the brush, these are the winds. . . .
Downstairs, you correct notes at the upright piano,
twice upright this midday Sunday torn from the whole
green cloth of summer; your room was once the laundry,
the loose tap beats time, you hammer the formidable
chords of *The Nocturne*, your second composition.
Since you first began to bawl and crawl
from the unbreakable lawn to this sheltered room, how often
winds have crossed the wind of inspiration—
in these too, the unreliable touch of the all.

14

5. *Harriet*

Spring moved to summer—the rude cold rain
hurries the ambitious, flowers and youth;
our flash-tones crackle for an hour, and then
we too follow nature, imperceptibly
change our mouse-brown to white lion's mane,
thin white fading to a freckled, knuckled skull,
bronzed by decay, by many, many suns. . . .
Child of ten, three quarters animal,
three years from Juliet, half Juliet,
already ripened for the night on stage—
beautiful petals, what shall we hope for,
knowing one choice not two is all you're given,
health beyond the measure, dangerous
to yourself, more dangerous to others?

Through the Night

Two buildings, scaffolds, go up across my street;
one owned by Harvard, the other owned by Harvard;
they keep on hammering from five till five.
Man shouting resounds on the steel ribs—
thus from a rib of the Ark and in his cups,
Noah harangued a world he said would drown. . . .
How could the reckless, authoritative young
bear me, if I had their life expectancy?
Their long hair, beads, jeans, are early uniforms—
like the generation of leaves, the race of man.
A girl straddles a car hood, and snuffs the dust of the headlights:
"I want to live," she screams, "where I can see."
The pale green leaf clings white to the lit night
and shakes a little on its stiff, tense twig.

2.

Nothing less nutritive than the thirst at Harvard—
it's as bad for me at fifty as nineteen—
the thirst for grown-ups, open cars and girls. . . .
While I was looking out a window
I saw you walking with the simple ones,
in the twilight, in the evening, in the black, in the night;
not painted or even loud—how earnestly,
I looked and found you lying on your bed;
you caught me and kissed me and stopped my rush,
your sinewy lips wide-eyed as the honeycomb,
we no longer needed to have lights.
On your record Alice Raveau's contralto
Orpheus sang, *Où vais-je sans Euridice?*
dying in our undergrowth, dense beyond reward.

16

3.

The vague, dark new hallway, the darker stairway:
closed doors to bathroom, bedroom . . . to someone waiting?
Your snoring is like the rub of distant surf,
each footstep is a moral sentence. The round window
holds out its thin, black terminal disk of joy,
the blissfully brightening glimmer of immoral
redemption as I lie awake basking,
trying to extend the dark and unspent minute,
as the window frame gradually burns green;
four panes assuming the polar blue of day,
as my backbone swims in the sperm of gladness,
as your figure emerges from your body,
we are two species, even from outside—
a net trapped in the arms of another net.

4.

Gradually greener in the window frame:
the old oil, unfamiliar here, alive
in a hundred eighteenth-century lawns and landscapes—
Sir Joshua Reynolds might improve each fault:
the lonely hound, the stalwart, cow-faced girl,
the scarlet general, more oaken than his oaks—
leaf, trunk and park arranged as if pretence
alone were sacred—sudden success or money
both being somewhat in bad taste at Harvard—
one great window, one bright watching eye;
as achingly I awake to steal back home,
each house and scaffold, familiar, unfamiliar—
each shingle-touselled window is sheer face . . .
blindingly visible breasts freckle to brilliance.

The Charles River

The sycamores throw shadows on the Charles,
as the fagged insect splinters, drops and joins
the infinite that scatters loosening leaves,
the long-haired escort and his short-skirted girl.
The black stream curves as if it led a lover—
my blood is pounding; in workaday times,
I take cold comfort from its heartelation,
its endless handstand round the single I,
the pumping and thumping of my overfevered wish. . . .
For a week my heart has pointed elsewhere:
it brings us here tonight, and ties our hands—
if we leaned forward, and should dip a finger
into this river's momentary black flow,
infinite small stars would break like fish.

2.

The circuit of snow-topped rural roads, eight miles
to ten, might easily have been the world's top,
the North Pole, when I trailed on spreading skis
my guide, his unerring legs ten inches thick in wool,
and pinched my earlobes lest they turn to snowdrops—
hard knocks that school a lifetime; yet I went on swiping
small things. That knife, yellow-snow with eleven blades,
where is it? Somewhere, where it will outlast me,
though flawed already when I picked it up. . . .
And now, the big town river, once straight and dead as its highway,
shrinks to country river, bankscrub, dry ice,
a live muskrat muddying the moonlight. You trail me,
Woman, so small, if one could trust appearance,
I might be in trouble with the law.

3.

No stars, only cars, the stars of man,
mount sky and highway; life is wild: ice straw
puts teeth in the shallows, the water smells and lives.
We walk a tightrope, this embankment, jewed—
no, yankeed—by highways down to a stubbly lip. . . .
Once—you weren't born then—an iron railing,
cheerless and dignified, policed this walk;
it matched the times, and had an esplanade,
stamping down grass and growth with square stone shoes;
a groan went up when the iron railing crashed. . . .
The Charles, half ink, half liquid coaldust,
bears witness to the health of industry—
wrong times, an evil dispensation; but who
can hope to enter heaven with clean hands?

4.

Seen by no visible eye, our night unbroken—
our motel bedroom is putty-gray and cold,
the shivering winds thrust through its concrete cube.
A car or two, then none; since midnight none.
Highways on three levels parallel the river,
roads patrol the river in her losing struggle,
a force of nature trying to breathe beneath
a jacket of lava. We lie parallel,
parallel to the river, parallel
to six roads—unhappy and awake,
awake and naked, like a line of Greeks,
facing a second line of Greeks—like them,
willing to enter the battle, and not come out . . .
morning's breathing traffic . . . its unbroken snore.

Harvard

1.

The parochial school's green copper dome is like
a green summer grove above the defoliated playground;
clouds puff in cotton wads on a low Dutch sky—
the top of the school resembles a Place des Vosges. . . .
Lying in bed, I see a blind white morning
rise to mid-heaven in a gaggle of snow—
a silk stocking is coiling on a wire hanger
rapier-bright . . . they dangle from my tree,
a long throw for a hard cold day . . . wind lifting
the stocking like the lecherous, lost leg. . . .
The students, my swarm-mates, rise in their hundreds, and leave
the hive—they can keep time. I've slept so late,
I see my stubble whiten while I shave;
the stocking blows to smog, the steel coathanger stains.

2.

We inch by the Boston waterfront on icepools,
carparks make the harbor invisible,
our relationship advances, then
declines to private jokes, the chaff of lust. . . .
Dark days, fair nights . . . yet they fell short—
in a studio near the Back Bay Station, the skylight
angular, night-bluish, blear and spinsterish—
both fighting off muscular cramps, the same fatigue. . . .
Yet tonight means something, something we
must let go willingly, and smash:
all flesh is grass, and like the flower of the grass—
no! lips, breasts, eyes, hands, lips, hair—
the overworked central heating bangs the frame,
as the milkhorse in childhood would clang the morning milkcan.

3. *Morning*

The great dawn of Boston lifts from its black rag;
from Thanksgiving to Christmas, thick arctic snow
thawing to days of moderate, night-black balm—
I cannot sleep, my veins are mineral,
dirt-full as the arteries of a cracked white cup;
one wearies of looking expectantly for the worse—
Chaucer's old January made hay with May.
In this ever more enlightened bedroom,
I wake under the early rising sun,
sex indelible flowers on the air—
shouldn't I ask to hold to you forever,
body of a dolphin, breast of cloud?
You rival the renewal of the day,
clearing the puddles with your green sack of books.

Sleep

1.

Four windows, five feet tall, soar up like windows,
rinsing their stained-glass angels in the void,
interminably alert for the four-hour stay till morning:
a watery dearth illuminated by
a light or two hung on a telephone pole;
an alley, ashcans, the usual Cambridge frame
clawed from packing crates, and painted dire,
frozen interminably to this four-hour verge. . . .
Heaven? The clock stops there as here—this flesh
elastic past the mind's agility,
hair coiled back on guard like the spring of a watch,
legs showing pale as wooden matches, lit
by four streak windows in the uncreating dawn
not night, not day, stealing brief life from both.

2.

Six straight hours to teach on less than three hours' sleep—
I shall be smitten by the hand of my cells,
and will not go down whiteheaded to my grave. . . .
I get to know myself, a spendthrift talker,
with no breath left to show in the last round. . . .
Back home, I sleep the hour hand round the clock
and enjoy the avarice of loneliness.
I lie like a hound, on bounds for chasing a hound,
short-tethered in a spare corner, nose on paws,
one eyelid raised to guard the bowl of water;
panting, "Better to die, than hate or fear,
better die twice than make ourselves feared or hated—
bad-livers live longer if the law's forgotten,
the happiest country has no history."

3.

An aquamarine bottle twinkles on a pane;
outside, a one-story factory with a troll chimney,
built in the age of novels and Fulton's steamboat,
condemned by law and Harvard, still on parole.
A tiger cat sentinelled on the record-player
spies on a second stretching from a carton-
dollhouse to bat a brass ball on a string.
The tree, untinselled, asymmetrical,
shoves up askewly blessing a small sprawl
of unsealed brownpaper Christmas packages.
Your child, she's nine, keeps shrewdly, inopportunely
reappearing—you standing up on your bed
in your Emily Dickinson nightgown, purely marveling
whether to be sensible or drown.

New York

1. *Snake*

One of God's creatures, just as much as you,
or God; what other bends its back in crooks
and curves so gracefully, to yield a point;
brews a more scalding venom from cold blood;
or flings a spine-string noosed about their throats:
hysterical bird, wild pig, or screaming rabbit?
Often I see it sunning on bright, brisk days,
when the heat has ebbed from its beloved rocks;
it is seamless, scaled-down to its integrity,
coiled for indiscriminate malevolence.
Lately, its valor pushed it past man's patience;
stoned, raw-fleshed, it finds its hole—sentenced
to hibernate fifty years. . . . It will thaw, then kill—
my little whip of wisdom, lamb in wolf-skin.

2. *Christmas Tree*

Twenty or more big cloth roses, pale rose or scarlet,
coil in the branches—a winning combination
for you, who have gathered them eight years or more:
bosom-blossoms from Caribbean steambath forests,
changeless, though changed from tree to tree, from Boston to here—
transplants like you. . . . Twenty small birds or more
nip the needles; a quail, a golden warbler—
the rest not great, except for those minnowy
green things, no known species, made of woven straw:
small dangling wicker hampers to tease a cat.
A fine thing, built with love; too unconventional
for our child to buy . . . to modesty
and righteousness of a woman's ego stripped naked:
"Because I lacked ambition, men thought me mad."

3. *New Year's Eve*

By miracle, I left the party half
an hour behind you, reached home five hours drunker,
imagining I would live a million years,
a million quarts drunker than the gods of Jutland—
live through another life and two more wives.
Life is too short to silver over this tarnish.
The gods, employed to haunt and punish husbands,
have no hand for trigger-fine distinctions,
their myopia makes all error mortal. . . .
My Darling, prickly hedgehog of the hearth,
chocolates, cherries, hairshirt, pinks and glass—
when we joined in the sublime blindness of courtship,
loving lost all its vice with half its virtue.
Cards will never be dealt to us fairly again.

4. *Dear Sorrow 1*

If I can't whistle in the dark, why whistle?
One doubts the wisdom of almighty God
casting weak husbands adrift in the hands of a wife.
We need the mighty diaphragm of Job
to jangle grandly. Pain lives in our free discussion,
like the Carlyles fighting meat from the mouth of their dog.
Luckily the Carlyles couldn't bear children—
ours sees me, "Genius, unwise, unbrilliant, weird,"
sees you, "Brilliant, unwise, unweird, nerves."
Barbaric cheek is needed to stay married. . . .
Lizzie, I wake to the hollow of loneliness,
I would cry out *Love, Love,* if I had words:
we are all here for such a short time,
we might as well be good to one another.

5. *Dear Sorrow 2*

Each day more poignantly resolved on love,
though the stars in their courses war against us . . .
I have climbed to the last step of the stairs to look:
an open window roughs the central heat,
my lackluster pictures, Holbein's *Sir Thomas More*
and Audubon's *Bluejays*, shine in the January air—
more cries of the city than that woodsman could name. . . .
If we have loved, it's not returnable;
this room will dim and die as we dim and die,
its many secrets change to others' things.
Can I be forgiven the life-waste of my lifework?
Was the thing worth doing worth doing badly?
Man in the world, a whirlpool in a river—
soul cannot be saved outside the role of God.

6. *Dear Sorrow 3*

We never see him now, except at dinner,
then you quarrel, and he goes upstairs. . . .
The old playground hasn't improved its asphalt base:
no growth, two broken swings, one OK—as was!
Our half century fought to stay in place.
But my eye lies, the precinct has turned hard,
hard more like a person than a thing.
Time that tinkers with objects lets man go,
no doctor does the work of the carpenter.
It's our nerve and ideologies die first—
then we, so thumbed, worn out, used, got by heart.
Each new day I cherish a juster perspective,
doing all for the best, and therefore doing nothing,
fired by my second alcohol, remorse.

7. *Dear Sorrow 4*

The hurt mother sleeps awake like a cat till daybreak
stretched on the mat by the bed of our breathy child . . .
her cat thrusts its small brown arm through a crack in the door,
then another arm, a brown nose, and the door sticks—
it is this waking daily to the fire of daybreak,
our twenty years of fractious will and feather. . . .
Do I romanticize if I think that I
can be as selfish a father as Karl Marx,
Milton, Dickens, Trotsky, Freud, James Mill,
or George II, a bad son and worse father—
the great lions needed a free cage to roar in. . . .
O when will I sleep out the storm, dear love,
and see at the end of the walk your dress glow
burnt-umber, as if you had absorbed the sun?

8. *Harriet's Dream*

"The broom trees twirped by our rosewood bungalow,
not wildlife, these were tropical and straw;
the Gulf fell like a shower on the fiber-sand;
it wasn't the country like our coast of Maine—
on ice for summer. We met a couple, not people,
squares asking Father if he was his name—
none ever said that I was Harriet. . . .
They were laying beach-fires with scarlet sticks and hatchets,
our little bungalow was burning—it
had burned, I was in it. I couldn't laugh,
I was afraid when the ceiling crashed in scarlet;
the shots were boom, the fire was fizz. . . . While sleeping
I scrubbed away my scars and blisters, unable
to answer if I had ever hurt."

27

9. *Term-End*   (*Harriet*)

The term is finished and the air is lighter,
I recognize your faces in the room;
I touch your pictures, find you in the round.
We watch a dark strip of silence stalk in rippling,
the singed back of your clingy Burmese cat;
he sits pointing the window from the bedspread,
hooked on the nightlife flashing through the curtain—
we cannot hold the focus for a minute. . . .
The beautiful cat gives his hideous purr to show
he wants us in the house, not back with God.
I want to live on long enough to see you
live longer than even the obliquest cat—
but to know you are happy would mean to lead
your life for you, hold hard, and live you out. . .

10. *Left out of Vacation*

"Some fathers may have some consideration,
but he is so wonderfully eccentric,
drinking buttermilk and wearing red socks.
It was OK—not having him in Florida;
Florence is different, Mother—big deal, two girls
eating alone in the Italian restaurant!" . . .
Only God could destroy the wonders He makes,
and shelve you too among them, Charles Sumner Lowell,
shiny horsechestnut-colored Burmese Cat,
waggling your literary haunches like Turgenev,
our animal whose only friends are persons—
now boarded with cats in a cat-house, moved at random
by the universal Love that moves the stars
forever rehearsing for the perfect comeback.

11. *The Picture*   (*Elizabeth*)

In New York, this is nature—twelve stories high,
two water tanks, tobacco-leaf shingle, girdled
by stapled pasture wire, while bed to bed,
we lie gazing into the ether's crystal ball,
sky and a sky and sky and sky, till death—
my heart stops . . . this might be heaven. At grandmother's
my terror of heaven was a scene from summer—
a picture, out of style now and then in,
of seven daffodils caught by the wind and still.
Buttercup yellow were the flowers, and green
the stems as fresh paint, over them the wind,
the blowzy wooden branches of the elms,
a sack of hornets sopping up the flame—
still over us, we still in parenthesis.

12. *Same Picture*

Still over us
high summer in the breath that overwhelms
the termites digging in the underpinning
down below
we two, two in one waterdrop
vitalized by one needledrop of blood,
up, up, up, up, and up
soon shot, soon slugged into the overflow—
and we two lying here,
one cell,
still over us our breath
sawing and pumping to the terminal,
no rest or stall
for the little wooden workhorse working here below.

Mexico

1.

The difficulties, the impossibilities . . .
I, fifty, humbled with the years' gold garbage,
dead laurel grizzling my back like spines of hay;
you, some sweet, uncertain age, say twenty-seven,
untempted, unseared by honors or deception.
What help then? Not the sun, the scarlet blossom,
and the high fever of this seventh day,
the predestined diarrhea of the pilgrim,
the multiple mosquito spots, round as pesos.
Hope not for God here, or even for the gods;
the Aztecs knew the sun, the source of life,
will die, unless we feed it human blood—
we two are clocks, and only count in time . . .
the hand a knife-edge pressed against the future.

2.

Wishing to raise the cross of the Crucified King
in the monastery of Emmaus at Cuernavaca—
the monks, world-names for futurist crucifixes,
and avant-garde Virgins . . . like St. Paul, they earned
the cost of depth-transference by learning a craft.
A Papal Commission camped on them two years,
ruling analysis cannot be compulsory,
their cool Belgian prior was heretical, a fairy. . . .
We couldn't find his corpse removed by helicopter;
the cells were empty, but the art still sold;
lay-neurotics peeped out at us like deer,
fatherless in spotless whitewashed cabins, named
Sigmund and *Karl*. . . . They live the life of monks,
one revelation healing the ravage of the other.

3.

The lizard rusty as a leaf rubbed rough
does nothing for days but puff his throat
on oxygen, and tongue up passing flies,
loves only identical rusty lizards panting:
harems worthy this lord of the universe—
each thing he does generic, and not the best.
We sit on a cliff like curs, chins pressed to thumbs—
how fragrantly our cold hands warm to the live coal!
The Toltec temples pass to dust in the dusk—
the clock dial of the rising moon, dust out of time—
two clocks set back to Montezuma's utopia . . .
as if we still wished to pull teeth with firetongs—
when they took a city, they murdered everything,
till the Spaniards, by reflex, finished them.

4.

South of Boston, south of Washington,
south of any bearing . . . I walk the glazed moonlight:
dew on the grass and nobody about,
drawn on by my unlimited desire,
like a bull with a ring in his nose, a chain in the ring. . . .
We moved far, bull and cow, could one imagine
cattle obliviously pairing six long days:
up road and down, then up again passing the same
brick garden wall, stiff spines of hay stuck in my hide;
and always in full sight of everyone,
from the full sun to silhouetting sunset,
pinned by undimming lights of hurried cars. . . .
You're gone; I am learning to live in history.
What is history? What you cannot touch.

5.

Midwinter in Cuernavaca, tall red flowers
stand up on many trees; the rock is in leaf.
Large wall-bricks like loaves of risen bread—
somewhere I must have met this feverish pink
and knew its message; or is it that I've walked
you past them twenty times, and now walk back?
The stream will not flow back to hand, not twice, not once.
I've waited, I think, a lifetime for this walk.
The white powder slides out beneath our feet,
the sterile white salt of purity and blinding:
your puffed lace blouse is salt. The red brick glides;
bread for a dinner never to be served. . . .
When you left, I thought of you each hour of the day,
each minute of the hour, each second of the minute.

6.

As if we chewed dry twigs and salt grasses,
filling our mouths with dust and bits of adobe,
lizards, rats and worms, we walk downhill,
love demanding we be calm, not lawful,
for laws imprison as much as they protect.
Six stone lions, allday drinkers, sit like frogs,
guarding the fountain; the three rusty arc-lights sweat;
four stone inkfish, much sat on, bear the fountain—
no star for the guidebook . . . this city of the plain,
where the water rusts as if it bled,
and thirteen girls sit at the barroom tables,
then none, then only twenty coupled men,
homicidal with morality and lust—
devotion hikes uphill in iron shoes.

7.

We're knotted together in innocence and guile,
yet we're not equal, I've lived too long without sense. . . .
Sounds of a popping bonfire; no, a colleague
typing; or is he needing paregoric?
The lavatory breathes out its sugared perfume
of Coca-Cola laced with rum. Tonight
in Cuernavaca, the night's illusory houselights
watch everyone, not just the girls, from houses
like boxes on main street where buses eat the sidewalk. . . .
It's New Year's midnight: we drink beer in the market
from cans garnished with limes and salt; one woman, Aztec,
sings adultery ballads, and weeps because
her husband has left her for three women—to face
the poverty all men must face at the hour of death.

8.

Three pillows, end on end, rolled in a daybed
blanket—elastic, round, untroubled. For a second,
by some hallucination of my hand
I imagined I was unwrapping you. . . .
Two immovable nuns, out of habit, too fat to leave
the dormitory, have lived ten days on tea,
bouillon cubes and cookies brought from Boston.
You curl in your metal bunk-bed like my child,
I sprawl on an elbow troubled by the floor—
nuns packing, nuns ringing the circular iron stair,
nuns in pajamas scalloped through their wrappers,
nuns boiling bouillon, tea or cookies, nuns
brewing and blanketing reproval . . .
the soul groans and laughs at its lack of stature.

9.

Next to last day baking on the marble veranda,
the roasting brown rock, the smoking grass, the breath
of the world risen like the ripe smoke of chestnuts,
a cleavage dropping miles to the valley's body;
and the following sick and thoughtful day,
the red flower, the hills, the valley, the Volcano—
this not the greatest thing, though great; the hours
of shivering, ache and burning, when we charged
so far beyond our courage—altitude. . . .
No artist perhaps, you see the backs of phrases,
a girl too simple to lose herself in words—
I fall back in the end on honest speech;
infirmity's a food the flesh must swallow,
feeding our minds . . . the mind which is also flesh.

10.

Poor Child, you were kissed so much you thought you were
      walked on;
yet you wait in my doorway with bluebells in your hair.
Those other me's, you think, *are they meaningless in toto,*
hills coarsely eyed for a later breathless conquest,
leaving no juice in the flaw, mind lodged in mind?
A girl's not quite mortal, she asks everything. . . .
If you want to make the frozen serpent dance,
you must sing it the music of its mouth:
Sleep wastes the day lifelong behind your eyes,
night shivers at noonday in the boughs of the fir. . . .
Our conversation moved from lust to love,
asking only coolness, stillness, conversation—
then days, days, days, days . . . how can I love you more,
short of turning into a criminal?

Eight Months Later

1. *Eight Months Later*

The flower I took away and wither and fear—
to clasp, not grasp the life, the light and fragile. . . .
It's certain we burned the grass, the grass still fumes,
the girl stands in the doorway, the red flower on the trees
where once the intermeshing limbs of Lucifer
sank to sleep on the tumuli of Lilith—
did anyone ever sleep with anyone
without thinking a split second he was God? . . .
Midsummer Manhattan—we are burnt black chips.
The worst of New York is everything is stacked,
ten buildings dance in the hat of one . . . half Europe
in half a mile. I wish we were elsewhere:
Mexico . . . Mexico? Where is Mexico?
Who will live the year back, cat on the ladder?

2. *Die Gold Orangen*

I see the country where the lemon blossoms,
and the pig-gold orange glows on its dark branch,
and the south wind stutters from the blue hustings;
I see it; it's behind us, love, behind us—
the bluebell is brown, the cypress points too straight—
do you see the house, the porch on marble pillars?
The sideboard is silver, and the candles blaze;
the statue stands naked to stare at you.
What have I done with us, and what was done?
And the mountain, El Volcan, a climber of clouds?
The mule-man lost his footing in the cloud,
seed of the dragon coupled in that cave. . . .
The cliff drops; over it, the water drops,
and steams out the footprints that led us on.

Circles

1. *Walk to the Barn*   (*Harriet*)

Nervous leaves twitter on the high wood elm,
this and that thing, grape-purple, skims the lawn—
our harmony is most alive and firm,
when three or four colors improve on black and white,
when six or seven words mean more than one . . .
Darling, this isn't us, I trapped in words,
you gagging on headoverheels inarticulation.
Or my barn . . . it's property uncouth as I.
Here nature seldom fears the hand of man,
the alders skirmish. You flame for a best friend—
is it always the same child or animal
impregnable in shell or coat of thorns,
punching you with embraces, holding out
a hestitant hand, unbending as a broom?

2. *Das ewig Weibliche*

Birds have a finer body and tinier brain—
who asks the swallows to do drudgery,
clean, cook, pick up a peck of dust per diem?
If we knock on their homes, they wince uptight with fear,
farting about all morning past their young,
small as wasps fuming in their ash-leaf ball.
Nature lives off the life that comes to hand—
if we could feel and softly touch their being,
wasp, bee and swallow might live with us like cats.
The boiling yellow-jacket in her sack
of felon-stripe cut short above the knee
sings home . . . nerve-wrung creatures, wasp, bee and bird,
guerillas by day then keepers of the cell,
my wife in her wooden crib of seed and feed. . . .

36

3. *Our Twentieth Wedding Anniversary* *1*   (*Elizabeth*)

Leaves espaliered jade on our barn's loft window,
sky stretched on a two-pane sash . . . it doesn't open:
stab of roofdrip, this leaf, that leaf twings,
an assault the heartless leaf rejects.
The picture is too perfect for our lives:
in Chardin's stills, the paint bleeds, juice is moving.
We have weathered the wet of twenty years.
Many cripples have won their place in the race;
Emmanuel Kant remained unmarried and sane,
no one could Byronize his walk to class.
Often the player outdistances the game. . . .
This week is our first this summer to go unfretted;
we smell as green as the weeds that bruise the flower—
a house eats up the wood that made it.

4. *Our Twentieth Wedding Anniversary* *2*

To our 20th. We live, two trees;
sometimes the green crack soonest in this soil
of granite and clamshells. Our first snapshot is still us,
ten or fifteen pounds inferior when
the Graces noosed you with my hard gold ring. . . .
The aging cling to life, even the dead do:
Rameses keeps the hair of a young squaw—
but where is Pharaoh the day after tomorrow?
By setting limits, man has withdrawn from the monsters;
a metal rod and then another metal rod;
when the old are dying, they buy land,
savings no consideration. . . . You dive me,
graceful, higher, quicker . . . unsteady swallow
who will uproot the truth that cannot change.

5. *The Human Condition* (*Harriet*)

The impossible is allied to fact—
should someone human, not just our machinery,
fire on sight, and end the world and us,
surely he'll say he chose the lesser evil—
our wars were simpler than our marriages,
sea monster on sea monster drowning Saturday night.
An acid shellfish cannot breathe fresh air. . . .
Home things can't stand up to the strain of the earth.
I wake to your cookout and Charles Ives
lulling my terror, lifting my fell of hair,
as David calmed the dark nucleus of Saul.
I'll love you at eleven, twenty, fifty,
young when the century mislays my name—
no date I can name you can be long enough.

6. *The Hard Way* (*Harriet*)

Don't hate your parents, or your children will hire
unknown men to bury you at your own cost.
Child, forty years younger, will we live to see
your destiny written by our hands rewritten,
your adolescence snap the feathered barb,
the phosphorescence of your wake?
Under the stars, one sleeps, is free from household,
tufts of grass and dust and tufts of grass—
night oriented to the star of youth.
I only learn from error; till lately I trusted
in the practice of my hand. In backward Maine,
ice goes in season to the tropical,
then the mash freezes back to ice, and then
the ice is broken by another wave.

7. *Words for Muffin, a Guinea-Pig*

"Of late they leave the light on in my entry,
so I won't scare, though I never scare in the dark;
I bless this arrow that flies from wall to window . . .
five years and a nightlight given me to breathe—
Heidegger said spare time is ecstasy. . . .
I am not scared, although my life was short;
my sickly breathing sounded like dry leather.
Mrs. Muffin! It clicks. I had my day.
You'll paint me like Cromwell with all my warts:
small mop with a tumor and eyes too popped for thought.
I was a rhinoceros when jumped by my sons.
I ate and bred, and then I only ate,
my life zenithed in the Lyndon Johnson 'sixties . . .
this short pound God threw on the scales, found wanting."

8. *Heat*

For the first time in fifteen years, a furnace
Maine night that would have made summer anywhere,
in Brazil or Boston. The wooden rooms of our house
dry, redoubling their wooden farmhouse smell,
honest wooden ovens shaking with desire.
We feared the pressure was too curative. . . .
Outside, a young seal festers on the beach,
head snapped off, the color of a pig;
much lonelier, this formula for cures.
One nostril shut, my other attenuated—
it's strange tonight I want to pencil myself
do-its on bits of paper. I must remember
to breathe through my mouth. Breathe only from my mouth . . .
as my mouth keeps shutting out the breath of morning.

Late Summer

1. *End of Camp Alamoosook*   *(Harriet)*

Less than a score, the dregs of the last day,
counselors and campers squat waiting for the ferry—
the unexpected, the exotic, the early
morning sunlight is more like premature twilight:
last day of the day, foreclosure of the camp.
Glare on the amber squatters, fire of fool's-gold—
like bits of colored glass, they cannot burn.
The Acadians must have gathered in such arcs;
a Winslow, our cousin, shipped them from Nova Scotia—
no malice, merely pushing his line of work,
herding guerillas in some Morality.
The campers suspect us, and harden in their shyness,
their gruff, faint voices hardly say hello,
singing, "Do we love it? *We love it.*"

2. *Familiar Quotations*   *(Harriet)*

A poet, if all else fail . . . your words from nowhere:
on your first visit to a child—"I am too happy,
sometimes the little muddler can't stand itself."
Your transistor was singing Anton Webern—
what is it like? Rugged: if you can like this,
you can like anything. "It's like red ants,
a wild wolf . . . through the woods walking—
or spiders crying together without tears. . . .
Who made God? Did God the Father take Baby
Jesus to Central Park on Sunday?" What's true?
Christ imagined all men were his brothers;
He loved all men, he was you, and might have lived—
for love, he threw his lovely youth away.
"But you can't love everyone, your heart won't let you."

40

3. *Bringing a Turtle Home*

On the road to Bangor, we spotted a domed stone,
a painted turtle petrified by fear.
I picked it up. The turtle had come a long walk,
200 millennia understudy to dinosaurs,
then their survivor. A god for the out-of-power. . . .
Faster gods come to Castine, flush yachtsmen who see
hell as a city very much like New York,
these gods give a bad past and worse future to men
who never bother to set a spinnaker;
culture without cash isn't worth their spit.
The laughter on Mount Olympus was always breezy. . . .
Goodnight, little Boy, little Soldier, live,
a toy to your friend, a stone of stumbling to God—
sandpaper Turtle, scratching your pail for water.

4. *Returning Turtle*

Weeks hitting the road, one fasting in the bathtub,
raw hamburger mossing in the watery stoppage,
the room drenched with musk like kerosene—
no one shaved, and only the turtle washed.
He was so beautiful when we flipped him over:
greens, reds, yellows, fringe of the faded savage,
the last Sioux, old and worn, saying with weariness,
"Why doesn't the Great White Father put his red
children on wheels, and move us as he will?"
We drove to the Orland River, and watched the turtle
rush for water like rushing into marriage,
swimming in uncontaminated joy,
lovely the flies that fed that sleazy surface,
a turtle looking back at us, and blinking.

41

5. *Winslows*

"Cousin Cal—if your Liz is Kentucky Derby,
she is strictly the root of the Southern rose.
Our dear Winslows—Auntie (Liz Ross Winslow)
is giving out at ninety-three this August;
Uncle John swallowed only one bite of roast beef
at his ninetieth birthday dinner last month;
Mother's cataract glasses are good, but she can't
see to paint, though she is only eighty-six;
only Aunt Daisy Anne at ninety-five plus
is *indominateable*. Don't worry,
I'm not going to be a poet, I haven't suffered.
I've left the *Ashville Globe*, journalism's for the public;
I've got to write for me. George will support me;
haven't all great artists had a patron?"

6. *Growth*   *(Harriet)*

"I'm talking the whole idea of life, and boys,
with Mother; and then the heartache, when we're fifty. . . .
You've got to call your *Notebook, Book of the Century*,
but it will take you a century to write,
then I will have to revise it, when you die."
Latin, Spanish, swimming half a mile,
writing a saga with a churl named Eric,
Spanish, Spanish, math and rollerskates;
a love of party dresses, but not boys;
composing something with the bells of *Boris*:
"UNTITLED, would have to be the name of it. . . ."
You grow apace, you grow too fast apace,
too soon adult; no, not adult, like us. . . .
On the telephone, they say, "We're tired, aren't you?"

42

7. *The Graduate*   (*Elizabeth*)

"Transylvania's Greek Revival Chapel
is one of the best Greek Revival things in the South;
the College's most distinguished graduate
was a naturalist, he had a French name like Audubon.
My sister Margaret, a two-bounce basketball
player and all-Southern Center, came home
crying each night because of 'Happy' Chandler,
the coach, and later Governor of Kentucky.
Our great big tall hillbilly idiots keep
Kentucky pre-eminent in basketball.
And how! Still, if you are somewhat ill-born,
you feel your soul is not quite first-class. . . ."
Never such shimmering of intelligence,
though your wind was short, and you stopped smoking.

8. *No Hearing 1. The Dialogue*

Old campaigner, we could surrender something,
not talking for a victory but survival;
quarrels seldom come from the first cause,
some small passage in our cups at dinner
rouses the Dr. Johnson in a wife—
a monologuist tries to think on his feet
while talking, maybe finds fine things, yet fails—
still, it's a privilege to earn the bullring.
We meet face to face in the 6 p.m. hour,
nursing two inches of family Bourbon
through two separate half-hours of television news,
heaven pumped in heartbeats to my head,
the red cherry rolling in the tumbler of sugared spirits . . .
in the days of the freeze, we see a minor sun.

9. *No Hearing 2. Alcohol*

I have been in the sun, and my lips keep twitching—
suddenly, no disinclination to murder—
these brown hours, they stream like water off my back.
I want to charge with bull-horns through the cedar hedge,
pretending left and right and wrong are wind. . . .
O to live in a small gone Horatian suburb
lost in its melancholy stream of traffic—
all for goodness, we both on in years. . . .
Mischievous fish-shapes without scale or eye
swim your leaf-green teagown, not maternal,
swirling six inches past your three-inch heel,
belling about you like a parachute—
Otello bellowing, the rug rolled up, a spate
of controversial spatter . . . then exhaustion.

10. *No Hearing 3*

Belief in God is an inclination to listen,
but as we grow older and our freedom hardens,
we hardly even want to hear ourselves . . .
the silent universe our auditor—
I am to myself, and my trouble sings.
The Penobscott silvers to Bangor, the annual V
of geese beats above the moonborne bay—
their flight is too certain. Dante found this path
even before his first young leaves turned green;
exile gave seniority to his youth. . . .
White clapboards, black window, white clapboards, black
        window, white clapboards—
my house is empty. In our yard, the grass straggles. . . .
I stand face to face with lost Love—my breath
is life, the rough, the smooth, the bright, the drear.

44

11. *No Hearing 4*

Discovering, discovering trees light up green at night,
braking headlights-down, ransacking the roadsides
for someone strolling, fleeing to her wide goal;
passing blanks, the white Unitarian Church,
my barn on its bulwark, two daytime padlocked shacks,
the town pool drained, the old lighthouse unplugged—
I watch the muddy breakers bleach to beerfroth,
our steamer, THE STATE OF MAINE, an iceberg at drydock.
Your question, my questioner? It is for you—
crouched in the gelid drip of the pine in our garden,
invisible almost when found, till I toss a white raincoat
over your sky-black, blood-trim quilted stormcoat—
you saying *I would prefer not*, like Bartleby:
small deer trembly and steel in your wet nest!

12. *Outlivers*   (*Harriet and Elizabeth*)

"If we could reverse the world to what it changed
a hundred years ago, or even fifty,
scrupulous drudgery, sailpower, hand-made wars;
God might give us His right to live forever
despite the eroding miracle of science. . . ."
"Was everything that much grander than it is?"
"Nothing seems admirable until it fails;
but it's only people we should miss.
The Goth, retarded epochs like crab and clam,
wept, as we do, for his dead child." We talk
like room-mates bleeding out the night to dawn.
"I hope, of course, you both will outlive me,
but you and Harriet are perhaps like countries
not yet ripe for self-determination."

13. *My Heavenly Shiner*   (*Elizabeth*)

The world atop Maine and our heads is north,
zeroes through Newfoundland to Hudson Bay:
entremets chinois et canadiens.
A world like ours will tumble on our heads,
my heavenly Shiner, think of it curving on?
You quiver on my finger like a small
minnow swimming in a crystal ball,
flittering radiance on my flittering finger.
The fish, the shining fish, they go in circles,
not one of them will make it to the Pole—
this isn't the point though, this is not the point;
think of it going on without a life—
in you, God knows, I've had the earthly life—
we were kind of religious, we thought in images.

14. *It Did*   (*Elizabeth*)

Luck, we've had it; our character the public's—
and yet we will ripen, ripen, know we once
did most things better, not just physical
but moral—turning in too high for love,
living twenty-four hours in one shirt or skirt,
breathless gossip, the breathless singles' service.
We could have done much worse. I hope we did
a hundred thousand things much worse! Poor *X's*,
chance went this way, that way with us here:
gain counted as loss, and loss as gain: our tideluck.
It did to live with, but finally all men worsen:
drones die of stud, the saint by staying virgin . . .
old jaw only smiles to bite the feeder;
corruption serenades the wilting tissue.

46

15. *Seals*

If we must live again, not us; we might
go into seals, we'd handle ourselves better:
able to dawdle, able to torpedo,
all too at home in our three elements,
ledge, water and heaven—if man could restrain his hand. . . .
We flipper the harbor, blots and patches and oilslick,
so much bluer than water, we think it sky.
Creature could face creator in this suit,
fishers of fish not men. Some other August,
the easy seal might say, "I could not sleep
last night; suddenly I could write my name. . . ."
Then all seals, preternatural like us,
would take direction, head north—their haven
green ice in a greenland never grass.

Obit

Our love will not come back on fortune's wheel—

in the end it gets us, though a man know what he'd have:
old cars, old money, old undebased pre-Lyndon
silver, no copper rubbing through . . . old wives;
I could live such a too long time with mine.
In the end, every hypochondriac is his own prophet.
Before the final coming to rest, comes the rest
of all transcendence in a mode of being, hushing
all becoming. I'm for and with myself in my otherness,
in the eternal return of earth's fairer children,
the lily, the rose, the sun on brick at dusk,
the loved, the lover, and their fear of life,
their unconquered flux, insensate oneness, painful "It was. . . ."
After loving you so much, can I forget
you for eternity, and have no other choice?